LIGHTING UP THE SKY

SHOOTING STARS

SETH KINGSTON

PowerKiDS press.
New York

Published in 2021 by The Rosen Publishing Group, Inc.
29 East 21st Street, New York, NY 10010

First Edition

Portions of this work were originally authored by Kristen Rajczak and published as *Shooting Stars*. All new material in this edition authored by Seth Kingston.

Editor: Elizabeth Krajnik
Book Design: Reann Nye

Photo Credits: Cover 4kodiak/E+/Getty Images; series art Zoteva/Shutterstock.com; series art Abstractor/Shutterstock.com; p. 5 Daniel Pludowski/EyeEm/Getty Images; p. 6 Lunaticm/Shutterstock.com; p. 7 Barcroft Media/Getty Images; p. 8 Carlos Fernandez/Moment/Getty Images; p. 9 Yongyut Kumsri/Shutterstock.com; p. 11 (top) Gary Friedman/Los Angeles Times/Getty Images; p. 11 (bottom) yousang/Shutterstock.com; p. 12 faboi/Shutterstock.com; p. 13 VW Pics/Universal Images Group/Getty Images; p. 15 Makarov Konstantin/Shutterstock.com; p. 16 Belish/Shutterstock.com; p. 17 SKY2015/Shutterstock.com; p. 19 Hyoung Chang/Denver Post/Getty Images; p. 21 Jasmine_K/Shutterstock.com; p. 22 MAV Drone/Shutterstock.com.

Library of Congress Cataloging-in-Publication Data

Names: Kingston, Seth, author.
Title: Shooting stars / Seth Kingston.
Description: New York : PowerKids Press, [2021] | Series: Lighting up the sky | Includes index.
Identifiers: LCCN 2019057163 | ISBN 9781725318571 (paperback) | ISBN 9781725318595 (library binding) | ISBN 9781725318588 (6 pack)
Subjects: LCSH: Meteors–Juvenile literature.
Classification: LCC QB741.5 .K56 2021 | DDC 523.5/1–dc23
LC record available at https://lccn.loc.gov/2019057163

Manufactured in the United States of America

CPSIA Compliance Information: Batch #CSPK20. For Further Information contact Rosen Publishing, New York, New York at 1-800-237-9932.

CONTENTS

LOOK UP!

If you look up into the sky on a clear night away from city lights, you'll probably see a few shooting stars. Shooting stars are some of nature's most beautiful light shows. Sometimes, shooting stars are called falling stars because they look like a star is falling out of the sky.

A shooting star is an **atmospheric** event called a meteor. People have observed and studied meteors for many years. In the mid-1800s, scientists discovered that meteors come from space. Read on to learn more about shooting stars, what causes them, and when to watch for them.

SEEING THE LIGHT

The word "meteor" comes from the Greek word *meteōron*, which means "high in the air." This is also the root for the word "meteorology," which is a science that deals with the atmosphere and weather.

This picture is of a bolide, which is a large meteor that usually explodes in a fireball.

WHAT CAUSES METEORS?

Bits of dust and rock that melt and fall off of **comets** each time they get close to the sun, called meteoroids, cause meteors. Small pieces of an **asteroid** can also form meteoroids. When meteoroids enter Earth's atmosphere, they burn up. This creates the streak of light in the sky we call a shooting star, or meteor.

When a meteor appears to be brighter than the planet Venus, the meteor is called a fireball. A photographer took this picture of a fireball during a meteor shower on August 14, 2016, in Terlingua, Texas.

A meteor often occurs when Earth moves into the path of solid **debris** a comet leaves behind. This is called the meteoroid stream. When meteoroids from the meteoroid stream enter Earth's atmosphere at high speeds, they create meteors.

BURNING UP!

Meteoroids that cause meteors may only be the size of a small rock or a grain of sand. However, they travel very fast! Meteoroids enter Earth's atmosphere at speeds ranging from 25,000 miles (40,234 km) per hour to 160,000 miles (257,495 km) per hour!

SEEING THE LIGHT

Meteoroids that enter the atmosphere at night tend to be slower, while meteoroids that enter the atmosphere during the day tend to be faster.

How fast a meteoroid enters Earth's atmosphere depends more on how much energy it has than on its mass. Most meteor-causing meteoroids are only 0.04 to 0.07 ounce (1 to 2 g).

Crashing into gas **molecules** causes the meteoroid to slow down and heat up. The meteoroid loses some of its energy to the gas molecules. They get rid of some of this energy as light, while the meteoroid glows and burns up. That's the light we see as a shooting star!

FALLING TO EARTH

Not all meteoroids burn up completely when they enter Earth's atmosphere. Meteoroids that fall to Earth are called meteorites. Meteorites can be as small as a pebble or as large as a boulder, or very large stone. However, they don't usually harm people.

Meteorites are separated into three groups: stony, **metallic**, and stony metallic. Stony meteorites are made of rocky material similar to what can be found on Earth. Most meteorites belong to this group. Metallic meteorites are made mostly of nickel and iron. Stony metallic meteorites are made of rocky and metallic material. Only about 8 percent of meteorites are metallic or stony metallic meteorites.

SEEING THE LIGHT

Scientists say that about 48.5 tons (44 mt) of meteoric **material** falls to Earth each day. However, it mostly falls into forests, the ocean, or in desert areas.

Scientists study meteorites to learn more about comets, asteroids, and what space was like billions of years ago. The materials in meteorites may even help scientists understand how life on Earth began.

METEOR SHOWERS

On any night of the year, meteors occur. Most nights, meteors occur as often as every 10 or 15 minutes. When there are a lot of meteors, that's called a meteor shower. A meteor shower can last for days. However, the shower's **intensity** will change from one day to the next.

SEEING THE LIGHT

Meteors that don't seem to be part of a shower are called sporadic meteors. These meteors come from six known sources, which only produce about five meteors per hour that can be seen with the naked eye.

Meteors often appear to come from the same point in the sky, called the radiant, because they enter Earth's atmosphere in **parallel** paths and at the same speed. Can you find the radiant in this photo?

We know that asteroids and comets are the source of most meteoroids. Meteor showers often occur at the same time every year, when Earth's orbit passes through a comet's orbit. Earth also passes through meteoroid streams that may have been created by a comet's orbit many years before.

THE PERSEIDS

The Perseids are an annual meteor shower, which means they happen once a year. They get their name from their radiant, which is the **constellation** Perseus. Meteor showers don't come from a constellation. This is just a guide for where in the sky people should watch for the meteors.

The Perseids come from debris from comet 109P/Swift-Tuttle, which takes 133 years to make one complete orbit around the sun. Perseid meteors travel at about 37 miles (59 km) per second. The Perseids reach peak activity during mid-August. At peak, you might be able to see up to 100 meteors per hour!

The Perseids are said to be the best meteor shower of the year. The fast and bright meteors are best viewed in the Northern **Hemisphere** during the hours before dawn.

RARE STORMS

Meteor storms occur when Earth's orbit passes through a recent comet's closely packed meteoroid stream. This doesn't happen often, which means meteor storms are rare. During a meteor storm, meteors often enter Earth's atmosphere in larger numbers and at faster speeds than they do during meteor showers.

The Leonid stream usually produces meteor storms every 33 years. Some years produce more intense storms than others.

One of the most memorable meteor storms of the last century came from the Leonid stream on November 17, 1966. On this night, about 40 meteors per second fell toward Earth for about an hour. Leonid meteors are very fast, traveling at about 45 miles (72 km) per second.

EYES TO THE SKY

People have watched meteor showers for centuries. Watching meteor showers is a great way to get out in nature and practice being an astronomer. Depending on where you live, what time of year it is, and the weather, you might be able to see a beautiful light show.

Most meteor showers are better viewed in the Northern Hemisphere than the Southern Hemisphere. This is because most meteors enter Earth's atmosphere in the Northern Hemisphere. The hours just before sunrise are the best time to view a meteor shower. Summer, fall, and early winter are the best seasons to watch for shooting stars.

SEEING THE LIGHT

Earth isn't the only planet to experience meteor showers. A planet just has to have a clear atmosphere to have meteor showers. However, these showers look different from how they look on Earth.

The Geminids, which have a radiant in the constellation Gemini, occur during mid-December. If you want to see a shooting star, the Geminids fall at a rate of about 60 to 70 meteors per hour at their peak.

GETTING READY

To watch a meteor shower, you must first find out when the next meteor shower is, when it'll be at peak, and what the weather and moon will be like on the peak night. Once you find out where in the sky the shower will occur, pick a place to watch the shower that's far away from lights, such as a state park, if you can.

Next, pack up the car. You'll want to bring blankets, pillows, camping chairs, things to do while you wait for the shower to start, and warm drinks. Make sure you dress for the weather!

Now you can lie back and wait for the show to begin!

BELIEFS ABOUT METEORS

- The ancient Greeks and Romans believed comets, meteors, and meteor showers meant something good or bad had happened or was going to happen.
- Some Eastern European peoples believed a meteor meant a man had escaped from prison or that someone had died.
- Some Native American groups believed meteors were the spirits of the dead or that war was coming.
- Today, some people say that if you see a shooting star that you should make a wish.

GLOSSARY

asteroid: A small, rocky body in space.

atmospheric: Of or relating to the atmosphere, which is the whole mass of air surrounding Earth.

comet: An object in outer space that forms a long, bright tail when it passes near the sun.

constellation: Any of 88 named groups of stars forming patterns.

debris: Broken pieces of objects or objects left somewhere because they're not wanted.

hemisphere: One-half of Earth.

intensity: The degree or amount of strength or force something has.

material: Something from which something else can be made.

metallic: Relating to, being, or looking like a metal.

molecule: The smallest possible amount of something that has all the characteristics of that thing.

parallel: Lying or moving in the same direction but always the same distance apart.

INDEX

WEBSITES

Due to the changing nature of Internet links, PowerKids Press has developed an online list of websites related to the subject of this book. This site is updated regularly. Please use this link to access the list:
www.powerkidslinks.com/lus/shootingstars